Tell Me the Story of JESUS

Tell Me the Story of JESUS

V. GILBERT BEERS

Illustrated by Cheri Bladholm

CANDLE
BOOKS

Published in 2004 by Candle Books
(a publishing imprint of Lion Hudson plc).

Distributed by Marston Book Services Ltd
PO Box 269, Abingdon, Oxon OX14 4YN

ISBN 1 85985 534 2

Worldwide coedition organised and produced by
Lion Hudson plc, Mayfield House, 256 Banbury Road,
Oxford, OX2 7DH, England.
Tel: +44 (0) 1865 302750 Fax: +44 (0) 1865 302757
Email: coed@lionhudson.com
www.lionhudson.com

Printed in Singapore

Contents

A Note to Parents

"Please tell me a story." "Please read me a story." How many times have you heard those requests? Children love a good story. They love to hear you tell or read a good story. As they listen, people and events come alive for them. The sound of your voice and the warmth of your presence add something special to the story.

The greatest story ever told is the story of Jesus. That's because his is the greatest life ever lived. But Jesus' greatness shows itself in his simplicity. Even a little child can relate to Jesus. It's easy for children to love him because they can easily see how much he loves them.

The story of Jesus is a story that attracts children to him. Your child will love Jesus more and more as you read this book together, or as your child reads it alone.

So this is the story of Jesus for children. But as you read it to your child, you will find yourself winsomely attracted to Jesus all over again. The childlikeness in your own heart will respond with your child to this story. You and your child will be bonded in a special way to Jesus and to each other.

V. Gilbert Beers

An Angel
Talks with Mary

Luke 1:26–38

"The Lord is with you, Mary!" The voice was like thunder. But it was also like sweet music. Mary had never heard a voice like that before. She was afraid.

Mary turned quickly to see who spoke. Then she was really afraid. An angel was standing there with her!

The angel looked something like a person. But he was shining like a bright light. This was a very important angel. He was one of the most important angels in heaven. His name was Gabriel.

"Don't be afraid," said Gabriel. "God has special plans for you, Mary. You will have a baby boy. He will be a great king forever."

"But how can I have a baby?" Mary asked.

Mary and Joseph were engaged. They planned to get married soon. But they were not married yet. So Mary and Joseph were not planning to have a baby now.

"God will be the baby's father," said Gabriel. "This baby will be God's Son."

"I will do whatever God wants," Mary answered.

Suddenly the angel was gone. Mary was alone again. But Mary had much to think about.

What would you have thought about if you were Mary?

An Angel
Talks with Joseph

᠕

Matthew 1:18–25

Mary and Joseph had big plans for their wedding. It was going to be a wonderful, exciting day. They were sure that after the wedding they would live together happily for the rest of their lives.

But that all changed for Joseph one day.

"Mary is going to have a baby!" Joseph whispered. "But this isn't my baby! How could this have happened? Who is the baby's father? What am I going to do?" Joseph was hurt. This changed everything.

Joseph could let people throw stones at Mary. That's what people did when a person had done something very wrong. And that's what Joseph thought Mary had done. But he loved Mary. He would not do that. He could make her stand in public and tell everyone what had happened. He would not do that either.

Joseph knew what he would do. He would quietly tell Mary to go away. They would never get married. Joseph was so sad and hurt.

Joseph was still thinking about this one night when he went to bed. He kept thinking and thinking about Mary. He loved her so much. Then Joseph went to sleep and began to dream.

Suddenly an angel stood there beside Joseph. The angel came to talk with Joseph about Mary. "Don't be afraid to marry her," said the angel. "God the Holy Spirit is the father of Mary's baby. The Scriptures said this would happen. You will name the baby Jesus. This means 'Saviour'. He will save his people from their sins."

Joseph woke up. He was so happy! Mary had not done anything wrong. She would have a special son. The baby would be God's Son.

So Mary and Joseph were married. Then they waited happily for the day when God's Son would be born.

You are happy about what happened to Mary and Joseph, too, aren't you?

Baby Jesus
Is Born

Luke 2:1–7

Mary and Joseph were so tired. It was a long trip to Bethlehem from their home in Nazareth. They did not have a car to ride in or a plane to fly in. That's because there were no cars or planes. And there were no trains or buses. Mary rode on a donkey. Joseph walked beside her. They were very happy when they came into the town of Bethlehem.

"We must find a place to sleep," said Joseph. "You might have your baby tonight."

Mary and Joseph went to the little inn. It was something like a hotel with no bedrooms or beds. It had no restaurant or snack shop either. But it did have places to lie down and sleep.

"Sorry, we have no room for you," said the innkeeper.

"But we must have somewhere to stay," said Joseph. "My wife might have a baby tonight."

The innkeeper looked at Mary. He felt sorry for her and Joseph. "You may stay in the stable with the animals," he said. "It isn't much. But it's all I have."

So that's where Mary and Joseph went. And that is where Mary had her little baby.

The animals watched sleepily as the new baby cried. They watched as Mary wrapped little Jesus in strips of cloth. And they watched her lay the little baby in the manger. That was the box where they ate their food.

Outside, the stars twinkled. The soft breezes blew gently. The people of Bethlehem were asleep by now. They did not know that people would sing about their little town many years later.

People will always remember Bethlehem. People will always remember that night when baby Jesus was born.

Shepherds Listen to an Angel Choir

Luke 2:8–20

A little lamb lifted its head and gave a sleepy "baaa". Nearby, a shepherd smiled. "Go to sleep, little lamb," the shepherd whispered. "Nothing exciting ever happens out here." The little lamb closed its eyes. So did the shepherd. For a while everything was very quiet.

Suddenly a bright line began to shine from the sky! The little lamb jumped up and looked around. So did the shepherd and his friends.

"An angel!" they shouted. They were afraid. You would be, too, wouldn't you?

"Don't be afraid," said the angel. "I have wonderful news for you. Tonight a baby was born in Bethlehem. He is God's Son. He is wrapped in strips of cloth and is lying in a manger."

Then the sky became brighter than any sky at noon. It was filled with a great choir of angels who began to sing. "Glory to God in the highest," they sang. "Those who please him will have peace." The shepherds could not even talk. No one on earth had ever heard a choir like this.

Then suddenly the sky grew dark again. It was quiet, except for the little lamb. "Baaa," said the little lamb.

"Let's go and see this baby," the shepherds shouted to each other. So they hurried to Bethlehem. There was the baby, just as the angels had said. "This is God's Son!" they whispered. Then they told everyone about the angel choir.

At last the shepherds went back to their sheep. They were so excited they could not sleep.

"Praise God!" they shouted.

"Baaa," said the little lamb.

The shepherds laughed. "I think he's praising God, too," said one of them.

Would you like to praise God just as the little lamb did?

Wise Men
Visit Baby Jesus

Matthew 2:1–12

In a land far away some wise men were watching the sky.

"Do you see the star?" asked one.

"Yes," said another. "It is the star of a special new king. He has just been born."

The wise men prepared for a long trip. They got onto their camels and rode for many miles. That was the best way to travel in those days. At last they came to Jerusalem.

"Where is the special new king?" the wise men asked some people.

Before long, King Herod heard what these men were asking. He did not like this. He did not want another king in the land. Herod wanted to be king. So he asked some religious leaders about this special new king. He asked where the new king would be born.

"In Bethlehem," they said. "That's what the prophets wrote in the Scriptures."

King Herod sent a message to the wise men. He asked them to come and see him.

"Go to Bethlehem," he said. "When you find this child, come back and tell me. Then I will go to worship him, too."

Herod did not want to worship Jesus. He wanted to get rid of him so he wouldn't grow up to be king.

The wise men followed the beautiful star to Bethlehem. They found the house where Mary and Jesus and the child Jesus were staying. They were so happy. They had found the special new king.

The wise men bowed down and worshipped Jesus. Then they gave him wonderful gifts. They gave him gold and spices called frankincense and myrrh. These gifts were worth a lot of money and would help take care of little Jesus for a long time.

The wise men were so happy as they went home. They had seen the new king. But they did not tell King Herod about Jesus. An angel had warned them not to do it.

If an angel told you not to do something, you wouldn't do it, would you?

Mary and Joseph
Take Jesus to Egypt

Matthew 2:13–23

An angel came to talk with Joseph after the wise men had left. He talked to Joseph in a dream.

"Take Jesus and Mary to Egypt," the angel said. "Jesus will be safe from King Herod there. Stay in Egypt until I tell you to come back."

So that night Joseph quietly slipped away from Bethlehem. He took Mary and Jesus to Egypt. They would be safe there.

King Herod soon learned that the wise men had gone home. They had not told him where to find Jesus.

Herod was angry. He sent soldiers to Bethlehem. He wanted them to find Jesus. He didn't want Jesus to grow up to be king. But the soldiers didn't find Jesus. He was gone.

That was a terrible time in Bethlehem. Everyone cried when the soldiers came.

At last King Herod died. The angel talked to Joseph in Egypt. He talked to Joseph in a dream. "It is time to go home," the angel said. "King Herod is dead."

But then Joseph heard that Herod's son was the new king. So he was afraid to go back to Bethlehem.

Joseph had another dream. Then he knew what to do.

"Now it is time to go home to Nazareth," Joseph said. That's where Joseph and Mary had lived before they went to Bethlehem. So Joseph and Mary and Jesus went to Nazareth to live. They were home at last.

Would you have liked to visit Mary and Joseph and Jesus in their home? What would you have asked them?

The Boy Jesus
Grows Up at Nazareth

∽

Luke 2:39–40

Joseph was a carpenter. Everyone who lived in the land of Israel in those days had a certain kind of work. Joseph made tables and chairs. He made wagon wheels and carts. He made just about anything that he could make from wood.

The people of Nazareth came to see Joseph when they wanted something made from wood. Joseph was a good carpenter, so he was very busy.

During the time when Jesus was growing up, each boy tried to learn about his father's work. Each boy helped his father do that work. So when Jesus was a boy he helped Joseph in his carpenter's shop.

Jesus learned to make many things from wood. He was a good carpenter, too.

Jesus grew to be a strong young man. People smiled when they listened to him talk.

"He is very wise," people would say.

"Yes," said Joseph. "He is a very wise boy."

God watched over his Son, Jesus. People could see that there was something very special about him.

Jesus spent time with Joseph and learned to be like him. But even more importantly, Jesus spent time with God, his Father in heaven, and learned to be like him.

You will spend time with your parents and learn to be like them. But even more importantly, you can listen to stories about God from the Bible. You can talk to God, your Father in heaven, and learn to be like him, too.

Jesus Teaches the Teachers

Luke 2:41–52

Every year people crowded into Jerusalem for the Passover holiday. It was like a big family reunion. Hundreds of families came to this big celebration. They talked. They ate. They worshipped the Lord. They went to God's house, the Temple. There was nothing quite as exciting as Passover.

When Jesus was twelve years old, he went to Jerusalem with Mary and Joseph. It was a wonderful time for them. Many of their neighbours were there. Many of their relatives were there. They all worshipped God at the Temple.

At last it was time to go home. In those days families and neighbours travelled together in a group called a caravan. They walked or rode donkeys or camels. That's all they had. There were no cars or trains or aeroplanes.

Mary and Joseph started for home in the caravan. Jesus was not with them. He was a big boy now. Mary and Joseph were sure he was with some neighbours or friends. But in the evening when they looked for him, they could not find him. Mary and Joseph began to worry. They went back to Jerusalem.

Mary and Joseph looked everywhere for Jesus. But they could not find him. Then they really were worried. "Where can he be?" they wondered.

Three days later they came to God's house, the Temple. There was Jesus, sitting with the great teachers. These great teachers knew a lot about God.

These teachers knew a lot about the first part of the Bible. The last part, which has these stories about Jesus in it, had not been written down then.

The teachers at the Temple were amazed at Jesus, this twelve-year-old boy. He knew as much as they did. He even knew more.

"Why have you done this to us?" Mary asked Jesus. "We have been very worried about you. We have looked everywhere for you."

Jesus smiled. "But you knew I would be in God's house, didn't you?" he asked.

Yes, Mary and Joseph should have known. Of course God's house was the right place to look for God's Son!

Your church is God's house also. It's a good place for you to go. When will you go there next?

John the Baptist Preaches

Luke 3:1–18

John the Baptist didn't go to a Baptist church. He didn't go to any church. That's because there were no churches in Jesus' time. Instead, people went to the synagogue in their town. People worshipped God in their synagogues every week. And for special holidays, they went to the Temple in Jerusalem.

John was called "the Baptist" because he baptised people. He put them into the water, and he quickly lifted them out of the water. When someone was baptised, that person was saying to others, "I have turned away from my dirty sins, Jesus made me clean from the sin in my heart."

John didn't look like a minister. He was a very rough-looking man. He lived out in the desert, where he ate locusts and wild honey. How would you like that for breakfast? John's clothes were rough, made from camel's hair. They probably looked like a big, hairy bathrobe. He wore a big, wide leather belt. You would be quite surprised if you saw someone like John preaching in church. You would be quite surprised if you saw someone like John anywhere!

John didn't preach like a minister either. He
walked through the desert, and he walked
along the Jordan River. He preached
outside. He had no pulpit or beautiful
building. He had no piano or organ or choir.

But there were some ways that John was
like ministers today. John told people they
must turn away from their sins. He said they must
turn to God. We do that today, too, don't we?

Many people listened to John preach. Some of them decided to turn from their
sins. They decided to turn to God and follow him.

If John the Baptist could teach a Sunday school class next Sunday, what do you think
he would say?

John
Baptises Jesus

Matthew 3:13–17

John the Baptist and Jesus were cousins. They were both grown men now.

One day Jesus went out to the place where John was preaching. It was by the Jordan River. Jesus wanted John to baptise him.

John knew that Jesus was God's Son. "I shouldn't baptise you," he told Jesus. "You should baptise me." Jesus must have smiled when John said that. It was true that Jesus was much more important than John. Jesus knew that. John knew that.

"I want you to baptise me," Jesus said. "It is the right thing to do."

So John and Jesus walked down into the water of the Jordan River. John baptised Jesus in the river. We don't know exactly how he did it. But we do know that after Jesus was baptised, he came up out of the water. So perhaps John held Jesus while he put him into the water and quickly brought him up again. Many people are still baptised that way today. Others are baptised by having water poured or sprinkled on their heads.

When Jesus came out of the water, heaven opened and the Spirit of God came down. The Spirit looked like a dove, and he landed on Jesus. Then God spoke from heaven. "This is my Son. I love him. I am very pleased with him."

Just think how great it would be to hear God say he is pleased with you!

Jesus was very special. He wasn't just Mary's son. He was God's Son. For hundreds of years people had waited for God's Son to come to earth. They called him "Messiah". Now he was here. Now he was ready to do wonderful things.

God's Son still does wonderful things. **He** *does wonderful things for you, too. You know that, don't you?*

Jesus Is Tempted

Matthew 4:1–11

After Jesus was baptised, the Holy Spirit led him into the desert. It was a lonely place with almost no plants or grass. There was no food to eat and no water to drink. Jesus stayed there for 40 days.

How long does it take for you to get hungry? Would you be hungry if you had nothing to eat for 40 days? Jesus was. He was very hungry. The Devil knew how hungry Jesus was. So he came to tempt Jesus to do wrong things.

"Look at all those stones around you," the Devil whispered. "They look like big loaves of bread, don't they?" The stones did look like loaves of bread. Looking at them made Jesus feel more hungry. "You can turn those stones into bread," the Devil said. "Do it! Then you can eat all you want."

"No," Jesus said to the Devil. "God's Word says that it is more important to obey God than to eat bread."

The Devil knew that Jesus had won against that temptation. God's Word always wins over the Devil.

Then the Devil took Jesus to the highest point on the Temple wall. "If you really are God's Son, jump off," the Devil said. "God's Word says that angels will catch you. Then people will know that you are God's Son for sure."

But Jesus answered, "God's Word says you must not try to test the Lord your God." The Devil had lost again. He could not fight God's Word.

The Devil tried one more temptation. He took Jesus to the top of a mountain. There he showed Jesus all the great kingdoms of the world. "These kingdoms are mine," the Devil told Jesus. "But I will let you rule them. All you must do is get on your knees and worship me."

"God's Word says you must worship God only," Jesus answered. The Devil had lost again. Jesus, with God's Word, had won again for the third and last time.

"Now get out of here," Jesus ordered. The Devil knew he could not get Jesus to sin. So he left. Then angels came and took care of Jesus.

When the Devil tries to get you to do wrong things, remember what Jesus did. He used God's Word against the Devil, and he won. You can, too!

Jesus'
First Followers

⁂

John 1:35–51

John the Baptist was standing with two men who followed him and learned from him. Then Jesus walked by, and John turned to look at him. "There is the Lamb of God," he told his two followers. John was telling them that Jesus was God's Son. He would die one day for their sins and for ours.

When John's followers heard who Jesus was, they left John. They followed Jesus instead. Jesus saw the two men. So he asked, "What do you want?"

"Where do you live?" the two men asked.

"Come with me," said Jesus. Then he took them to the place where he was staying. The men talked with Jesus from four o'clock until the end of the day.

One of the two men was Andrew. He went to find his brother, Simon.

"We have found God's Son, the Messiah," he told Simon. So Simon went with Andrew to see Jesus.

Jesus said, "You are Simon. But you will be called Peter, which means 'rock'."

The next day Jesus left for Galilee and asked Philip to come along. Philip ran

first to find his friend Nathanael. "We have found God's Son, the Messiah," he said. "He is Jesus, from Nazareth."

Nathanael laughed. "Nazareth? Can anything good come from that town?"

"Come and see," said Philip.

Soon Philip and Nathanael were near the place where Jesus was waiting.

"Here comes an honest man," Jesus said about Nathanael.

"How do you know that?" Nathanael asked.

"I could see you sitting under the fig tree before Philip found you," said Jesus.

"You really are God's Son," said Nathanael.

"You will see greater things than that," said Jesus. "You will even see heaven open, and angels will be coming back and forth to me."

If you saw angels with Jesus, what would you say? Would you believe that he is God's Son?

Jesus Turns
Water into Wine

∽

John 2:1–12

Jesus and his mother, Mary, were invited to a wedding at Cana. Jesus' new followers were asked to come, too. It was a wonderful wedding, as most weddings were in those days. It was like a big party. But the party went on and on. Before long the host ran out of wine. Mary came to see Jesus about this.

"You shouldn't ask me to help," Jesus said. "It's not my time to start doing miracles."

But Mary told the servants, "Do whatever Jesus tells you."

There were six big, clay pots standing nearby. Each one held about 90 to 135 litres. "Fill them with water," Jesus told the servants. "Then take some to the man in charge of the wedding."

The servants did exactly what Jesus said. That's always a good idea, isn't it? When the man in charge of the wedding tasted the water, it wasn't water at all. It had become wine!

"This is wonderful," he said to the bridegroom. "This is the best wine you have served at your wedding party!"

That was Jesus' first miracle. People who saw it knew that he was not an ordinary man. They knew he must be God's Son to do a miracle like that. Jesus' followers had seen this miracle, too. Now they were sure that he was God's Son.

Would you like to have been at the wedding party with Jesus? It's always special to be with Jesus, isn't it?

Jesus Talks
with Nicodemus

John 3:1–21

One night a Jewish religious leader came to see Jesus. His name was Nicodemus. "Teacher, your miracles prove that God has sent you to teach us," Nicodemus said.

Jesus looked at Nicodemus. He knew what Nicodemus had come for. Nicodemus had come to learn about heaven. He wanted to know how to get there.

"You must be born again," Jesus said to Nicodemus. "Then you will be part of God's Kingdom."

Jesus' answer surprised Nicodemus. "How can an old man be born a second time?" he asked. "Can he go back inside his mother and be born once more?"

"No, that's not it," Jesus explained. "Do you hear the wind?" Nicodemus listened. The wind was whispering among the trees.

"Where did it come from?" Jesus asked. "Where is it going?"

Nicodemus did not know. No one does.

"God's Spirit moves among people this way," Jesus said. "The Holy Spirit will give a person a new life. Getting this new life is like being born a second time."

This was hard for Nicodemus to understand. Jesus told him, "You are a great teacher, but you must learn what I am saying. I will be lifted up on a cross. I will do this so people who believe in me can be born again."

Then Jesus said these beautiful words to Nicodemus. "God loved the world so much that he gave his only Son. Anyone who believes in me will live forever. God sent me to save people from their sins."

Would you like to say thank you to Jesus now for coming to earth for you? He would love to hear you say that.

Jesus Talks with a Woman at a Well

John 4:1–42

Jesus and his friends had been walking all morning. There were no cars or trains or aeroplanes then, so most people walked. Like Jesus, they walked many, many miles.

Jesus and his friends were tired and hungry. It was lunchtime. You're usually hungry by lunchtime, aren't you? You would be very hungry if you had walked all morning.

Jesus sat by a big stone well. People came to this well to get water. They couldn't pump the water or turn on a tap. They had to let a jug or bucket down into the well with a rope. Then they pulled up the jug or bucket filled with water.

While Jesus sat there, his friends went into a nearby village. They went to buy some lunch. While they were gone, a woman came to the well. She wanted to get some water.

"May I have a drink of water?" Jesus asked. The woman was surprised. She was

a Samaritan woman, and Jesus was a Jewish man. Jewish people never talked to Samaritan people. They hated Samaritans.

But Jesus didn't hate anyone. He loved all people. The woman didn't know that, so she said to him, "Why are you asking me for a drink?"

Jesus may have really needed a drink of water. But he knew that the woman needed water, too – a special kind of water that only he could give her.

"You really should ask *me* for water," Jesus said. "I could give you living water. If you drink my living water, you will never be thirsty again." Jesus was telling the woman about the new life he can give.

As Jesus and the woman talked, she began to see that he was no ordinary man. He was God's Son. So the woman ran home. She wanted to tell her friends and neighbours. Before long, many friends and neighbours came to meet Jesus. Many of them believed that he was God's Son. They believed that he had come to save them from their sins.

"Please stay for a while," the new believers begged. So Jesus and his friends stayed for two days. While they were there, many others believed in him. They became his followers.

Would you like to help some friends follow Jesus, too?

Jesus Calls
Four Fishermen

❧

Mark 1:16–20

Simon Peter and some friends were fishing one day when Jesus arrived. He wanted to talk with Simon Peter and his brother, Andrew. These two fishermen were tossing their nets into the lake. They pulled the nets towards them. They were hoping to catch fish.

Jesus watched them for a while. Then he spoke. "It's time to stop fishing," he said. "It's time for you to follow me. We will fish for people." Jesus was talking about helping people come to God. That can be even more fun than fishing.

So Simon Peter and Andrew dropped their nets. Now it was time to stop fishing. Now it was time to follow Jesus. So they walked along the shore with Jesus.

Before long Jesus and his two new followers saw James and John. They were Zebedee's sons. They also fished for a living.

James and John were in a boat. The two brothers were fixing their nets. "It's time to stop fishing," Jesus told them. "It's time to follow me." So they dropped their nets and followed Jesus.

Now Jesus had four followers. These were his first four.

As time went on, Jesus found eight more followers. Then he had twelve of them. Sometimes we call these twelve men "disciples". That's because they followed Jesus and learned from him.

Someday the disciples would do great things for Jesus. But for now they had to stay with him. They had to learn many things from him. Then they could do his work.

Before they worked for Jesus, the disciples learned from Jesus. That's good for us to remember, isn't it?

Catching Fish
with Jesus

Luke 5:1–11

One day Jesus preached a sermon. But he wasn't behind a pulpit. He stood on the shore of the Sea of Galilee. This was a big, beautiful lake. Many people crowded around Jesus. They squeezed closer and closer. Before long they almost pushed Jesus into the water.

Jesus saw two empty boats nearby. The fishermen who owned the boats were there, too. They were washing their nets. One of these men was Simon Peter.

Peter and some friends had decided to follow Jesus. But sometimes they still went fishing.

Jesus climbed into Simon Peter's boat. He asked Simon Peter to push the boat away from the shore. Then Jesus sat in the boat. He preached to the people on the shore.

"Let's go fishing," Jesus said when he finished preaching. "When you get farther out on the lake, let your nets down into the water. You'll catch many fish in the nets."

Simon Peter looked tired. "We have fished all night," he said. "We did not catch one fish. But we will do whatever you say." So they did. Simon Peter and his friends took their boats out onto the lake. They let down their nets.

Suddenly the water was splashing with dozens of fish. They swam right into the nets! Soon the nets were full of these fish.

When the fishermen hauled their nets in, the fish filled the boats. Peter and his friends looked at Jesus. They knew he had made this happen.

Then Simon Peter got down on his knees in front of Jesus. He was sure now that Jesus was God's Son. No ordinary man could have done this.

"From now on, you will follow me," Jesus said. So when they landed, they decided to leave everything. From now on, they were going to follow Jesus.

You will keep on following Jesus, too, won't you?

A Hole in the Roof

Mark 2:1–12

People everywhere were hearing the good news that Jesus could heal people. So everywhere Jesus went, crowds came. They wanted him to help them.

One day Jesus came to a town called Capernaum. People pushed and shoved to get near to Jesus when he went into a house. Soon the house was full of people.

So Jesus preached to these people. While he was preaching, four men arrived with a friend. They were carrying this friend on a stretcher. That's because the man was paralysed. He could not walk. He could not even move.

But there was no way for the men to get into the house. What could they do? They were sure that Jesus would heal their friend if they could just get near him. Then one of them had a great idea. They climbed up to the roof of the house. This roof wasn't like the one on your house. It was made of clay, and it was flat.

The people dug through the clay. They made a big hole in the roof. Then they let their friend down through the hole. They let him down on his stretcher. Then he was in front of the place where Jesus was standing.

Jesus felt sorry for this man. He saw how the man and his friends believed in him. "Your sins are forgiven," Jesus said to the paralysed man.

Some religious leaders were standing nearby. They didn't like what Jesus had said. "Only God can forgive sins," they grumbled. They were whispering. But Jesus knew what they were saying.

"I am God's Son," he said. "I have the power to forgive sins. Watch! I will prove that I have this power. I will heal this man. Then you will know that I can forgive sins, too!"

So Jesus talked to the paralysed man. "Stand up. Pick up your stretcher," he said. "Walk home. You are healed."

The man jumped up. He walked through the crowd. He was carrying his stretcher. You know how surprised those people were, don't you? No one else could heal a paralysed man. Jesus was certainly God's Son. "Praise God!" they shouted.

Can you say, "Praise God"?

Jesus Asks Matthew to Follow Him

Matthew 9:9–13

Matthew was a tax collector. Each day he sat in a little booth beside the road. Jewish people came to him to pay their taxes. Most people don't like to pay taxes. But those people hated to pay their taxes. That's because the money went to the Romans. They were the foreign people who ruled over the Jewish people.

Jewish people hated tax collectors like Matthew, too. The tax collectors were Jewish themselves, but they collected the taxes for the Romans. You see now why Matthew's neighbours hated him, don't you?

One day Jesus came down this road. He saw Matthew sitting in his little booth. He watched Matthew collecting taxes from people. He saw how people hated Matthew. But Jesus didn't hate Matthew. He loved Matthew. Jesus loves everyone.

"Follow me!" Jesus said to Matthew. So Matthew the tax collector left his little booth. He had decided to follow Jesus. He would never be a tax collector again. From that time on, he would be Jesus' disciple. We know Matthew best for writing the book of Matthew in the Bible.

Later that day Jesus and his friends went to Matthew's home for dinner. Matthew invited other tax collectors to the dinner, too. He wanted all of them to believe in Jesus.

But some of the Jewish religious leaders were angry about this. "Why does Jesus eat with people who have done such bad things?" they grumbled.

Jesus heard them. "I came from heaven to help sinners know God," he said.

Jesus wants to help you and me know God, too. Will you let him?

Jesus Calls Twelve Disciples

Mark 3:13–19; *Luke* 6:12–16

Jesus loved to pray. That's because he loved to talk with his heavenly Father. Do you like to pray, too? When you do, think how wonderful it is to talk with God.

One day Jesus went up on a mountain to pray. Jesus kept on praying. He prayed all night.

At last it was morning. Jesus called all his followers together. He chose twelve of them to be his special disciples. They were sometimes called apostles. Jesus wanted these twelve to be very close to him. They would stay with him every day. They would listen to him. They would learn all they could from him.

The twelve disciples, or apostles, would also preach for Jesus. They would even help to heal people. Jesus would give them special power. He would let them do things that only he could do.

John   James   Matthew   Simon   Bartholomew   Philip
                                                     (Peter)   (Nathanael)

49

| Andrew | Judas Iscariot | James (son of Alphaeus) | Judas (Thaddaeus) | Simon (the Zealot) | Thomas |

Here are the names of these twelve.

There was Simon, also called Peter, and his brother, Andrew.

There were James and John, who also were brothers.

Four more were named Philip, Bartholomew, Matthew, and Thomas.

Then there was another James. He was the son of Alphaeus.

And there was another Simon. He was a member of the Zealots. That was a group of people who worked hard for something they thought was right. They worked hard to stop the Romans from ruling over the Jewish people.

Then there was a man named Judas. He was also known as Thaddaeus. His father's name was James.

There was also another man named Judas. His last name was Iscariot. Later Judas Iscariot turned against Jesus and betrayed him.

These twelve disciples learned to do many special things for Jesus. Matthew, John, and Peter even wrote some of the books in the Bible.

Don't you wish you could talk with these men? Would you like to ask them about following Jesus? They could tell you wonderful things, couldn't they?

Jesus Heals
an Officer's Servant

Luke 7:1–10

"Your servant is almost dead," some other servants told a Roman army officer. The Roman officer was very important. He was in charge of 100 other soldiers.

The officer looked very sad. This servant was very special to him. Some people thought servants were not important. But the Roman officer thought they were important. He was a very kind man. He loved his servant. How could he lose him?

Then the officer heard that Jesus was coming. Jesus was just outside Capernaum. That's the town where the Roman officer lived.

So the officer asked some important Jewish leaders to find Jesus. "Beg Jesus to heal my servant," he said. The Roman man had been kind to these leaders. So they were happy to help him.

Before long the leaders found Jesus. "Please come and heal this man's servant," they begged. "This Roman army officer is a good man. He loves us. He even built a synagogue for us."

Jesus went with the Jewish leaders. He was on his way to the officer's house. He was going to heal the servant. But along the way some of the officer's servants met them. The officer had sent them.

"The Roman officer says you should not come to his house," they said. "He said to tell you he is not worthy for you to be there. Just speak a word and his servant will be healed."

Jesus was amazed. "I haven't seen this much faith in our own Jewish people," he said. The army officer was Roman. The Jewish people thought the Romans did not believe in God. They were called pagans. That means "ungodly people". But here was an important Roman man trusting in Jesus. So Jesus sent them home. The servant would be healed.

The men that the officer had sent to Jesus went home. There they found the servant completely well! Jesus had healed him without touching him. He had healed him from far away!

Do you think the Roman officer believed Jesus was God's Son now? You would, wouldn't you?

Jesus Stops a Storm

Mark 4:35–41

"Let's go across the lake," Jesus said to his disciples. The lake was called the Sea of Galilee. So Jesus and his friends got into a boat. They started out across the lake.

Soon a terrible windstorm came. The wind howled as it came down from the hills. The waves on the water grew higher and higher. No one should be out in this kind of storm. Before long, water from the lake began to fill the boat.

Jesus was sleeping in the back of the boat. His head rested on a cushion. But Jesus' friends weren't sleeping. They were so scared! They woke Jesus. "Teacher!" they shouted. "We're going to drown! Don't you care?"

Of course Jesus cared. But he wanted to show his disciples once more that he was God's Son. He wanted to show them that he was no ordinary man. So Jesus spoke to the wind and the waves. "Be quiet!" he ordered. The wind obeyed him like a little child. It became very still. The big waves on the water died down quickly. Soon the lake was completely calm. There wasn't even a little ripple on the water.

"Why were you so afraid?" Jesus asked. "Don't you believe in me yet?"

Jesus' friends stared at him. They could hardly talk. They were filled with wonder. "Who is this man?" they whispered. "Even the wind and waves obey him."

No ordinary man could make wind and waves obey him. Only God's Son could do that.

You believe Jesus is God's Son, don't you?

Jesus Heals Jairus' Daughter

Matthew 9:18–26; Mark 5:21–43

Jesus had just stepped out of the boat. He had come from the other side of the Sea of Galilee. The crowds were waiting for him on the shore. But one man rushed from the crowds. He ran towards Jesus.

"Please help me!" the man begged. "My little daughter is very sick. I'm afraid she will die."

Jesus looked at this man. His name was Jairus. He was an important leader of the synagogue in town. That's the place where people went to worship God each week. Many of the religious leaders of that time did not like Jesus. Some even hated him. But Jairus believed that Jesus could help him and his little girl.

"Please come and heal my daughter," the man begged. "Please help her live." So Jesus went with Jairus.

But suddenly Jesus stopped. "Someone touched my clothes," he said. Jesus' disciples were surprised. The crowds were pushing and shoving to be near him. Why was he asking about one person who touched him? But Jesus stood still. He waited.

Then a woman stepped towards him. She was afraid. The poor woman had been sick for twelve years. She had gone to many doctors. She had spent most of her money. But no one had helped her. But as soon as she touched Jesus' clothes, she was well!

The woman was trembling. What would Jesus say? What would he do? "Your faith has healed you," Jesus said. "From now on you will be well." You know how happy that woman was, don't you?

Jairus was watching all of this. He was waiting for Jesus to come home with him. But at that moment some people came from his house. "It's too late," they said. "Your daughter is dead."

Jesus looked at Jairus. He saw how sad the man looked. "Don't be afraid," Jesus said. "Trust me."

Then Jesus took Peter, James, and John with him. He made the crowd stay outside. Jesus and his three friends went with Jairus and his wife to the girl's room. Jesus put the girl's hand in his and spoke. "Get up, little girl," he said. The girl, who was twelve years old, jumped up and walked around the room! How excited and how happy her parents were! Jesus told them to give their daughter something to eat.

What do you think Jairus and his wife said to Jesus then? What would you have said to Jesus?

Jesus Feeds 5,000 People

Matthew 14:13–21; *John* 6:1–15

One day Jesus sailed across the Sea of Galilee again. When he reached the other side, the crowds were waiting. That's what happened wherever Jesus went. Some of these people were going to Jerusalem for the Passover holiday. Some wanted Jesus to heal them. Others wanted Jesus to heal friends or family members. Others just came to watch.

Wherever Jesus went, the crowds went, too. On this day Jesus went up into the hills. The crowds went up into the hills, too. They stayed there with Jesus all afternoon.

When it was time for dinner, Jesus' disciples didn't know what to do. The crowds of people had not brought anything to eat, and the disciples had nothing to give them.

"We have nothing for these people to eat," the disciples told Jesus. "Send them away so they can find some food."

"No," Jesus said. "You feed them."

Philip looked at all of the people. He said, "We don't have enough money to buy food for so many people."

Then Andrew saw that one person had brought food. A little boy had five little loaves of bread, like buns. He had two little dried fish. Andrew told Jesus about the lunch. "But that's all there is," Andrew said. "We can't feed thousands of people with that!"

"Tell everyone to sit down," Jesus said. "It's time for dinner." So 5,000 men sat down on the grass. All the women and children sat down, too.

Jesus took the little loaves of bread. He held the two little fish. And he thanked God for them. Then he began to break the bread and fish into pieces. All of the people there ate until they were full. There were even 12 baskets of leftovers!

When the people saw this, they were amazed. Jesus had taken one little lunch and made it into enough for more than 5,000 people! How could Jesus do this? Who was he? "Surely he is God's Son," they said.

They were right. Jesus is God's Son, isn't he?

Jesus Walks on Water

Matthew 14:22–33

After Jesus fed the 5,000 people, he sent them home. Then he told his disciples to go across the Sea of Galilee. Jesus stayed there alone on the hillside to pray.

As the disciples crossed the lake, it became dark. Night was coming, and a storm was coming too. The wind began to blow harder and harder. Before long, the waves were very high, just as they had been on the night when Jesus was sleeping in the boat. The disciples were struggling to get their boat across the lake.

About three o'clock in the morning the disciples saw something strange. It looked as if a man was walking on the stormy lake. But how could that be? "It's a ghost!" some of them screamed.

Then they heard a voice saying, "Don't be afraid." It looked like Jesus walking across the lake. He was walking on top of the stormy waves!

"Is it really you, Jesus? If it is, let me walk out on top of the water to meet you," Peter shouted.

"Come on," said Jesus.

So Peter climbed over the side of the boat. He began to walk on the water towards Jesus. Then he looked around at the high waves. As soon as he did that, he felt afraid and began to sink into the water. "Save me!" Peter cried out to Jesus.

Jesus reached out to Peter and lifted him up. "Why did you doubt me?" Jesus asked. "Where is your faith?"

Jesus and Peter climbed into the boat. When they did, the wind stopped. The disciples worshipped Jesus. They were amazed. "Surely you are God's Son," they said.

Of course we know that he is, don't we?

Jesus Heals a Blind Man

∽

Mark 8:22–26

One day Jesus and his friends came to Bethsaida. It was a little village, but big crowds of people were already there. Wherever Jesus went, crowds squeezed close to him. Many people begged Jesus to heal them.

In Bible times there were almost no doctors or nurses. There were no hospitals or clinics. When people got sick, they often stayed sick for a long, long time. Many of them died. They had no one to help them.

There was a blind man in this little village. He could not see the beautiful things that other people saw. Can you see beautiful things? Perhaps you do *not* see very well. You may even be blind. Then you know how this man felt.

The blind man's friends brought him to Jesus. They asked Jesus to help him. "Please touch him!" they begged. "Please heal him."

Jesus felt sorry for the man. He wanted to help him. So Jesus reached out. He took the blind man's hand in his. Then he led the man away from the village.

Jesus put his own spit on the blind man's eyes. Then Jesus placed his hands on the man. "Do you see anything now?" Jesus asked.

"Yes, I see people!" the man said. "But I can't see them very well. They look like trees walking around."

Jesus put his hands over the man's eyes again. Suddenly the man could see everything. He was completely healed! He was so happy! You would be happy if Jesus helped you the way he helped that man, wouldn't you?

"Go home to your family!" Jesus told the man.

What do you think the man did then?

Jesus Shines
like a Bright Light

Luke 9:28–36

Jesus loved to pray. He often went to a quiet place. There he would talk with God, his Father in heaven. You like to do that too, don't you?

If you had been one of Jesus' disciples, would you have liked to listen to Jesus pray? Of course you would!

Peter, James, and John were three of Jesus' disciples. They were his special friends, and they liked to hear Jesus pray, too. So Jesus often took them with him.

One day he went up on to a hill to pray. His three special friends went with him. But Peter, James, and John felt sleepy. Soon they went to sleep.

While Jesus was praying, his face began to shine. His clothes began to look like a bright light.

Then two other men stood with Jesus. They were Moses and Elijah, who had been dead for hundreds of years. Now they came back from heaven to talk with Jesus. They were shining, too. That's because they had been in heaven for so long.

What do you think these two men said to Jesus? They talked about the way

Jesus was going to die in Jerusalem. He was going to die for everyone, even you and me. Jesus did that so that we can go to live with him in heaven someday.

Peter, James, and John woke up and looked around. Suddenly they were wide awake! They saw Jesus shining like a bright light. They saw Moses and Elijah as they were leaving.

"Let's build three little tents from sticks and leaves," Peter shouted to Jesus. "You can have one. Moses and Elijah can each have one." Of course Jesus didn't need a little tent. Neither did Moses or Elijah.

Suddenly a bright cloud came over them. Peter, James, and John were afraid.

The three disciples wondered what was happening. Then a voice came from the cloud. It sounded like thunder. But it also was beautiful, like music.

"Jesus is my Son!" the voice said. It was God's voice! "I have chosen him to do my work! Listen to him." Now you know why you and I should listen to Jesus, don't you?

The voice became quiet. Moses and Elijah were gone. Everything was quiet. No one was there with Peter, James, and John except Jesus. But those three disciples had seen something special. No other person had ever seen this before. Now Jesus' three special friends were sure that Jesus was God's Son. God had said so himself.

When God tells you in the Bible that Jesus is his Son, you believe him, don't you?

Who Is the
Greatest Person
on Earth?

Matthew 18:1–6; Luke 9:46–48

Have you ever heard someone say, "I'm the greatest"? You would never say something like that, would you?

Some of Jesus' friends almost said that. One day the disciples came to Jesus. "Which of your friends will be the greatest in heaven?" they asked. Actually each one of them was hoping that Jesus would say, "You will be!" But he didn't.

The disciples had even been arguing about this earlier. Jesus knew what they were thinking. He knew that each one wanted to be the greatest.

So Jesus asked a little child to come over to him. Jesus' friends wondered what he was going to say. What did he want with a child?

"You must become like this little child," Jesus said to his friends. "If you don't, you won't get to heaven."

Jesus' friends were surprised. How could they become like a little child?

"Turn from your sins," Jesus said. "Turn to God. Become childlike." Jesus' friends had seen many people try to act importantly. The disciples were learning that Jesus doesn't want his friends to do that. They must be humble. That's the way Jesus was on earth. He didn't act like an important person.

"You must be friends with little children," said Jesus. "When you are friends with them, you are my friend, too. But don't ever cause a little child to sin. If you do, you will be punished. And you'll wish that you weren't around anymore."

Jesus loves children very much. You know that, don't you?

Jesus Visits
Mary and Martha

Luke 10:38–42

Mary and Martha lived in Bethany. That was like a little suburb of Jerusalem. The two sisters and Jesus were good friends.

One day Jesus and his disciples came to town. So they stopped to see Jesus' friends. Martha was there at the door to welcome them.

Mary sat down on the floor. She wanted to hear everything Jesus said.

Martha had no time to listen. She was worried about making a big dinner.

So Martha hurried to the kitchen. You should have heard the pots and pans clanging as Martha worked! But Martha wasn't happy. She was working so hard while Mary was just sitting close to Jesus, listening to him.

Martha stomped over to Jesus, who was talking to Mary. "Look at my sister sitting beside you, doing nothing," Martha grumbled. "I'm working so hard to get dinner. Is that fair? Tell Mary to come and help me!"

"My dear friend Martha," Jesus said. "You're spending all your time getting dinner. Mary is spending her time talking with me. What she is doing is better."

We don't know what happened next. But Jesus may have asked Martha to sit down and listen to him talk. Later, perhaps all of them had a simple lunch together.

Who needs a big dinner when we can talk with Jesus?

Jesus Is the Good Shepherd

John 10:11–18

Do you have neighbours who are shepherds? If you live on or near a farm, you may know some shepherds. But many people have never seen a shepherd. In Bible times there were many shepherds. That's because there were many sheep. Someone had to take care of them.

Jesus said, "I am the Good Shepherd." Did Jesus take care of sheep? Did he stay out in the fields with sheep? What was Jesus saying?

Jesus was saying that we are his sheep and he takes care of us. If you're a little child, you are Jesus' little lamb. He is your Good Shepherd. He helps you get good food to eat just like shepherds help their sheep find good food. Jesus helps you have water to drink and a place to stay. He helped your parents find the home where you live. He takes care of you and your family every day.

"I know my sheep," Jesus said. He knows your name. He knows when you cut your finger. He knows when you are hungry or thirsty. He knows when you are afraid. Jesus knows all about you.

"I give my life for my sheep," Jesus said.

Jesus died on the cross for you. That's because he loves you so very much. He wants you to live with him someday in his home. That's heaven, you know.

Would you like to ask Jesus to be your Saviour? He wants to be your Saviour. But you must ask him. He wants to be your Good Shepherd, too.

Jesus Helps
Lazarus Live Again

John 11:1–44

Lazarus was very sick. His sisters, Mary and Martha, sent someone to find Jesus. They wanted Jesus to heal Lazarus.

Jesus loved Mary and Martha and their brother, Lazarus. But he did not go to their house for two days. Even then his disciples were afraid. "Some of the people around there want to kill you," they said.

"We must go," Jesus told them. "Lazarus has gone to sleep. I must go and wake him." The disciples were surprised. Why did Jesus need to go to Bethany to wake his friend?

Then Jesus told them that Lazarus was not just sleeping. "Lazarus is dead," he said. "Now you will see what I do. When you see it, you will believe in me."

Mary and Martha lived in Bethany, which was near the big city of Jerusalem. At last Jesus and his disciples came toward the house. Many people were there, crying and moaning. That was a way to show how sad they were. Martha ran out to meet Jesus.

"You should have come before!" Martha said to Jesus. "Then Lazarus would not have died."

"Your brother will live again," Jesus told Martha.

"Yes, I know he will live in heaven someday," she answered.

Then Jesus said, "People who believe in me will die like everyone else, but they will live again."

Martha went home to get her sister, Mary. Jesus and the two sisters and all their friends went to the tomb where Lazarus was laid.

"Roll that big stone away from the doorway of the tomb," Jesus commanded.

Martha was afraid. "Lazarus has been dead for four days," she said. "His body will be rotting and smelling." But the people did what Jesus said.

When the stone was rolled away, Jesus prayed, "Thank you, Father, for hearing me." Then Jesus shouted, "Lazarus, come out!"

People stared at the tomb. What would happen? Then they saw Lazarus, wrapped in strips of cloth. He was walking out toward them. Many who saw this believed that Jesus was God's Son. Who else could help a dead person live again?

Could you?

Jesus Heals
Ten Lepers

Luke 17:11–19

Jesus and his friends were going to Jerusalem. Along the way, they went into a little village. There they saw ten men with leprosy. That was a terrible disease. People with leprosy had big sores. Sometimes part of their skin fell off. Lepers could not live with friends and family. People were afraid they would catch this disease.

The ten men cried out to Jesus. "Help us!" they begged. "Please heal us."

"Find a priest," Jesus said. "Show him that you are healed."

The men still had their big sores. But they believed that they were healed. They knew that their sores would go away if they obeyed Jesus. So they hurried to find a priest and, as they went their sores disappeared. Their leprosy was gone!

One man turned around and went back to Jesus. That man was a Samaritan. He was part Jewish and part foreigner. Most Jewish people hated the Samaritans.

"Thank God!" the man shouted. "I'm healed." Then he bowed down by Jesus' feet. He thanked Jesus for healing him.

"Weren't there ten men with leprosy?" Jesus asked the people around him. "Where are the other nine?"

Then Jesus spoke to the man who had come back. "You are healed because you believe in me," he said. "You may go now. You are well."

Has Jesus done something special for you? Would you like to say thank you to Jesus now?

Jesus Loves Children

Mark 10:13–16

Does Jesus love children? Or is Jesus too important for children? Does he have time to listen to you? Listen, and you'll find out!

One day some mothers and fathers saw Jesus. He was doing important things. He healed people. He helped blind people see. He helped deaf people hear. He even brought dead people back to life! No one was more important than Jesus.

The fathers and mothers wanted Jesus to bless their children. Would he put his hands on them? Would he say something special to them? Would anyone doing such important work take time for children?

The parents brought their children to Jesus. They asked him to bless their children.

But Jesus' disciples tried to send the parents away. You can imagine what they were saying. "He's too busy for little children. He doesn't have time for little children. Go away!"

Jesus saw what the disciples were doing. He didn't like that at all! Jesus loved the children. He still does!

"Let the children come to me," Jesus said. "Don't send them away. God's Kingdom belongs to these little children."

Then Jesus said, "Anyone who comes to God must come like a little child. If a person doesn't do that, he or she can't get into heaven."

Jesus took the children into his arms. He said some very special things to them. They were very happy. They could tell how much Jesus loved them. Their parents were happy too. They were glad that Jesus loved their children and wanted to be with them.

Do you ever feel that Jesus is holding you in his arms? Does it ever seem that he is saying special things to you? He loves you very much, you know. You love him, too, don't you?

A Rich Young Man
Asks about Heaven

Matthew 19:16–30

"Teacher, what good things must I do to live forever?" a young man asked Jesus. The young man was asking how he could go to heaven. We all want to know that, don't we?

"Why are you asking me about what is good?" Jesus asked. "God is the only one who is good." Did the young man really know that Jesus was God's Son? Perhaps he did. Perhaps that is why he was asking Jesus about heaven.

Then Jesus told the young man how to get to heaven. "Obey God," Jesus said. "Do what God tells you to do. Obey God's rules."

The young man thought about that. "Which rules?" he asked. The young man didn't understand. It's not enough just to obey *some* of God's rules. We must obey *all* of God's rules.

Jesus didn't get upset. He was very patient as he named a few rules. He began with the Ten Commandments. "Don't kill people. Don't pretend another person's husband or wife is yours. Don't steal. Don't lie. Honour your father and mother. Love your neighbour as you love yourself."

"I've obeyed all of those rules," the young man said. "What else?"

Jesus could have told him about hundreds of other rules. No one has obeyed all of them. Even the young man could not have obeyed every one. But Jesus didn't do that. He wanted to test the young man's love for God. The young man said he *obeyed* God. But did he really *love* God?

"Now you're asking how to be perfect," Jesus said. "If that's what you want, sell everything you have. Give the money to poor people. Then come and follow me."

The young man thought about all his money and things. He didn't want to give them up. He would obey rules. But he wouldn't give up his money. He loved God. But he didn't love God *that* much. So he turned sadly and walked away.

If you could talk to that young man, what would you like to say to him?

Jesus Heals Bartimaeus

~~~

Mark 10:46–52

There were many, many blind people in Jesus' time. That's because people sometimes were not careful about keeping clean. Also people then did not have good medicine. And there weren't many doctors to help them. So Jesus and his friends often saw blind people in the crowds.

Jesus was leaving Jericho with his disciples. Crowds of people followed him just as they always did. Some hoped to be healed. Some hoped that Jesus would heal a friend or family member.

A man named Bartimaeus sat beside the road. He was sitting there alone. No one else was there to help him. People in the crowd were not thinking about Bartimaeus. They were thinking about themselves or about friends. But Bartimaeus heard that Jesus was coming by. So he began to shout. "Help me, please!" he shouted. "Be kind to me, Jesus."

Some people nearby yelled at Bartimaeus. "Be quiet!" they said. Poor Bartimaeus. No one seemed to care. Would Jesus care?

"Tell Bartimaeus to come here," Jesus said. Some people told Bartimaeus what Jesus had said. Bartimaeus threw off his ragged coat. He felt his way over to Jesus.

"What do you want me to do?" Jesus asked.

"Please help me see," Bartimaeus answered.

"All right," said Jesus. "You can see! Because you believe in me, you are healed."

Suddenly blind Bartimaeus was not blind anymore. He could see! He was so excited and so happy! He must have walked around telling everyone, "I can see! I can see!"

Then he followed Jesus.

Would you follow Jesus if he did something special for you? Has he?

Little Zacchaeus
Climbs a Big Tree

୬◔ଡ଼

Luke 19:1–10

No one liked Zacchaeus. That's because no one liked tax collectors. They made people pay taxes. That's always hard to do. But these taxes went to the Romans. They were the foreign people who ruled the land. Zacchaeus worked for the Romans, so none of the Jewish people liked him. Even Zacchaeus may not have liked himself. If he was ashamed of the work he did, he was probably ashamed of himself, too.

One day Zacchaeus heard that Jesus had come to Jericho. That's the town where Zacchaeus lived. Zacchaeus ran to find Jesus, it wasn't hard to find him, there was always a crowd of people around Jesus.

But Zacchaeus had a problem. All the people crowding around Jesus were much taller than he was. Zacchaeus was a short little man. How could he talk to Jesus? He couldn't even see Jesus.

Then Zacchaeus had a good idea. He ran down the road ahead of Jesus and the crowd. He climbed a big sycamore tree. He climbed out on a big limb. He knew

Jesus would walk under this limb. And he knew he would be able to see Jesus then.

That is exactly what happened. When Jesus came by, he looked up into the tree. He must have smiled to see Zacchaeus up there. "Come down, Zacchaeus," Jesus said. "I want to come to your house today."

Zacchaeus was so happy. He climbed down from the tree as fast as he could. Then he took Jesus to his house.

Some of the people didn't like that. How could Jesus visit such a bad man?

"From now on, I will give half of my money to the poor," Zacchaeus said to Jesus. "If I have cheated people, I will give each one of them four times as much as I took."

Jesus was pleased. He said, "This shows how God has changed your life, Zacchaeus. I came to earth to find lost people like you. I am here to help lost people find God."

Do you know any children who need Jesus? Would you like to tell them about Jesus?

Mary Pours Perfume
on Jesus' Feet

John 12:1–8

Do you remember Mary and Martha and Lazarus? These two sisters and one brother lived in Bethany, a little village near Jerusalem. Jesus had been to their home before. Once when he came to visit, Martha kept busy getting dinner. But Mary listened to Jesus talk about God, his Father in heaven.

On another trip, Jesus arrived after Lazarus had died. It was a very sad time. But Jesus told Lazarus to come back to life again. He did!

Now Jesus had come to visit again. Lazarus was there with Mary and Martha. He was alive and well. This time Jesus came six days before the Passover holiday. Families came from everywhere for this big family celebration in Jerusalem. They ate and sang. They talked together. They worshipped God together. Jesus was going to the holiday celebration.

Mary, Martha, and Lazarus were glad Jesus had stopped to visit them on his way to Jerusalem. They loved Jesus. So they had a big dinner for him. They wanted to honour Jesus. He had done so much for them.

After dinner Mary brought a jar with perfumed oil to the table. When she opened it, the sweet smell filled the house. This jar cost a lot of money. Mary poured the perfumed oil on Jesus' feet. Then she wiped his feet with her hair. She wanted to honour Jesus. She wanted to show him how special she knew he was. This was her way of doing it.

A disciple named Judas grumbled. "That stuff is worth a lot of money," he said. "She could have sold it. She could have given the money to poor people." Judas wasn't really thinking about poor people. He wanted the money himself.

"Leave her alone!" Jesus told Judas. "You can always help poor people. But Mary won't always be able to honour me this way. I won't be with you much longer." Jesus knew that he would die in Jerusalem. He would die for you and me.

If Jesus came to your house, what special gift might you give him? What kind thing might you do for him?

Jesus Rides into Jerusalem

Matthew 21:1–11

There is a beautiful hill east of Jerusalem. In Jesus' time it was covered with olive trees. So it was called the Mount of Olives. That's a good name for it, don't you think?

One special day Jesus and his disciples were on the Mount of Olives. While they were there, Jesus sent two disciples into a little nearby village. "When you go into the village, you will see a donkey tied there," Jesus told them. "A young colt will be with the donkey. Bring them here to me. Someone may ask what you are doing. Just say that I need the donkey and its little colt."

The disciples did what Jesus asked. They brought the donkey and its colt to Jesus. They put their coats on the little colt's back. Jesus would ride on it. Many people threw their coats on to the path. The little colt would walk over them. Some people cut tree branches. They put the branches on the path.

Crowds pushed ahead of Jesus. Crowds pushed behind him. Many squeezed in close on each side of him. They began to shout. "God bless King David's son," they shouted. "Praise God! Praise God in the highest heaven."

The whole city of Jerusalem heard this noise. "Who is coming?" people in the city asked.

The people in the crowd around Jesus shouted, "Jesus is coming!"

Don't you wish you could have seen this? Don't you wish you could have been there? What would you have shouted? What would you have said to Jesus?

Jesus Talks
about a Coin

Mark 12:13–17

Everyone should like Jesus. But some people don't. Some even hate him. That's because Jesus makes us think about our sin. That's the bad stuff we have done. He wants us to turn away from our sin. He wants us to turn to God.

When Jesus lived here on earth, some of the Jewish religious leaders hated him. That's because Jesus came to turn people to God. The religious leaders did not like that. They wanted people to follow them. They thought they were important.

One day some religious leaders tried to trick Jesus. They wanted him to say something wrong. Then they could tell people how terrible he was. "You always tell the truth," these people said. "So should we pay taxes to Rome or not?"

It was a trick question. What if Jesus said the people should pay taxes to Rome? That would make the people angry at him. They did not want to pay taxes to Rome. But what if Jesus said they should not pay taxes to Rome? Then he would get into trouble with the Roman government. Was Jesus trapped? What would he say?

"Show me a coin," Jesus said. "Then I will tell you." The men gave a coin to Jesus.

"Whose picture is this on the coin?" Jesus asked.

"Caesar's," they answered. Caesar was like a king. He was called "emperor". He was the most powerful person on earth at that time.

"If this is Caesar's money, give it back to him," Jesus said. "But give God what belongs to him."

The trick was over. The people did not know what to say. They knew that Jesus was right.

You know that Jesus was right, too, don't you? You know he is always right.

A Poor Widow Gives
More than Rich People

❧

Luke 21:1–4

Jesus and his disciples were in the city of Jerusalem. They were in God's house. It was called the Temple. This was a very large stone building with many courtyards. Jesus and his disciples were in the courtyard where people gave their offering money. They dropped their money into boxes that looked like trumpets.

Rich people came in. They looked around. They wanted to be sure others were watching them. Then they dropped lots of money into the offering boxes. People would often say good things about the rich people. "Look how much that person gave!" "He gave more than the last two people together."

Then a woman came in. She was a widow, for her husband was not alive anymore. She was poor, too. She did not have much money. But she dropped in two small copper coins. None of the people said good things about her. How could they? She didn't give much.

But Jesus said good things. "That poor widow gave more than all of the rich people together," Jesus said. His disciples were surprised. How could Jesus say that? She had given almost nothing.

"Those rich people gave what they didn't need," Jesus said. "That poor widow gave all she had."

Think about that the next time you give to God. Are you giving what you don't need? Or are you giving what you would really like to keep?

Jesus' Last Supper

Mark 14:12–26

The Passover was beginning. It was the first day. People had come to Jerusalem from everywhere. They talked together. They ate together. They laughed. They prayed. They went to God's house, the Temple, together. This first day was a special day. It was a time when people gave lambs as offerings to God.

These offerings reminded the people of the first Passover. That was when the Israelites left Egypt hundreds of years ago. That night the angel of death passed over each house that had blood sprinkled over the door. The oldest son was safe in each of these Israelite houses. But the Egyptians lost their oldest sons. So Pharaoh finally let the Israelite slaves go free. That's why the people, who were now called Jews, celebrated Passover every year. They kept remembering that wonderful night long ago.

Jesus and his disciples were going to eat the Passover supper together. So Jesus sent two disciples to prepare it. "You will find a man carrying a pot of water," Jesus said. "Follow him home. Talk to the man who owns the house. He will take you to a large upstairs room. Prepare our supper, and we will eat together there."

Everything happened as Jesus had said. So the two disciples made the Passover supper. That evening Jesus and all twelve of his disciples ate the supper together. They lounged on big benches around the table. That's the way people ate in those days.

"One of you will turn against me and betray me," Jesus said. "But it will be sad for that person." The disciples wondered who it would be. They did not know that it would be Judas.

Jesus took some bread and thanked God for it. Then he broke it into pieces. He gave a piece to each disciple. "Eat this," he said. "This is my body." Then he took the cup of wine. He  thanked God for it. Then he gave it to the disciples. Each drank some of it. "This is my blood," Jesus said. "I will give my blood for many." Jesus was telling his disciples that he was going to die for them. He also died for us. He did this to save us from our sins so we can get to heaven.

This would be a good time for you to thank Jesus. It would be a good time to ask him to be your Saviour.

Jesus Prays in a Garden

Matthew 26:36–57; Luke 22:39–54

The Passover supper was over. Jesus and his disciples left the upstairs room. They walked across the city of Jerusalem. They crossed the big valley east of the city. Then they climbed up the Mount of Olives. There was a beautiful garden on this hill. It was filled with olive trees. It also had some big rocks. It was called Gethsemane.

Jesus went to a quiet place to pray. Most of his disciples stayed behind. But he took Peter, James, and John close to the place where he was going. "I am so sad and crushed," Jesus told them. "Stay awake while I pray."

Jesus went a short distance away from his three special friends. He began to pray. "Father, do I have to suffer this way? Do you have another way? But I want to do what you want." Jesus knew that he would have to die on the cross. It made him feel so terrible that he began to sweat big drops of blood.

Then Jesus went back to Peter, James, and John. They were sleeping! "You should get up now," Jesus said. "Pray that you won't give up when you are tempted to do wrong."

Jesus prayed three times. The third time that he went back to the disciples, Judas suddenly came into the garden. He had a mob with him. These people had clubs and swords. The religious leaders had sent them. Judas had told these men that he would greet Jesus. Then they would know the person to capture. So Judas went over to Jesus. "Hello, teacher," he said. Then he hugged Jesus. He gave Jesus a kiss on the cheek.

"How can you turn me over to this mob with a kiss?" Jesus asked.

Jesus' disciples were afraid of the mob. They all turned and ran away. Then Jesus was alone. So the men with Judas captured Jesus. They took him back into the city of Jerusalem.

But you would never run away from Jesus, would you? He would never run away from you when you need him.

Peter Denies
That He Knows Jesus

Matthew 26:57–58, 69–75; *Luke* 22:54–62

The mob that captured Jesus took him to the high priest. The high priest was the most important religious leader in the land.

Peter followed the mob to the high priest's home. But he waited in the outside courtyard. Jesus was taken inside the house.

Peter was sitting by a fire in the courtyard. It was a chilly night. Several people were there. One of them was a servant girl.

"You were with Jesus," she said.

"I don't know what you're saying," Peter argued.

Later another servant girl saw Peter. "This man was with Jesus," she told the others.

"I don't even know the man," Peter shouted. This time he swore that he didn't know Jesus.

Still later some other people came to Peter. "We know you are one of Jesus' disciples," they said. "We heard you talk, and we could tell that you are from

Galilee." Peter was afraid. He didn't want to suffer with Jesus.

Peter cursed and swore. "I don't know the man," he shouted. Just then a rooster crowed. Then Peter remembered something Jesus had said. "Before the rooster crows, you will deny me three times." At that very moment some men led Jesus past Peter. Jesus turned and looked at him.

Peter had never felt so sad before. He ran from the courtyard as fast as he could go. He was so sorry that he had denied knowing Jesus. The big, rough fisherman began to cry. He cried and cried until he thought his heart would break.

If you had been there, what might you have said to Peter?

Jesus Is Taken
to Pilate and Herod

Matthew 27:11–31; *Luke* 23:1–25; *John* 18:28–40

The religious leaders kept Jesus all night. Early the next morning they took Jesus to Pilate. He was the Roman governor.

"So what's this man done wrong?" Pilate asked. "Why are you bringing him here?"

"We want you to nail him to a cross. Kill him."

Pilate wanted to talk with Jesus. "Are you the King of the Jews?" he asked.

"I am not a king on earth," Jesus said. "I am a king, but my Kingdom is not in this world."

Pilate wanted to set Jesus free. But the religious leaders shouted and argued. They wanted to kill Jesus.

Then Pilate had an idea. He sent Jesus to see Herod, who was in Jerusalem at the time. King Herod ruled Galilee, where Jesus lived. Perhaps Herod could have Jesus killed. Then Pilate would not have to do it.

Herod was happy to see Jesus. He had heard of Jesus' miracles. But he thought

they were just magic tricks. He wanted Jesus to do a magic trick for him. But of course Jesus would not do that. So Herod and his men began to make fun of Jesus. Herod put a king's robe on Jesus. Then he sent Jesus back to Pilate.

Pilate tried again to set Jesus free. But the religious leaders argued too much.

"I'll let you have one prisoner," Pilate said. "You may have Jesus or Barabbas." Barabbas was a terrible murderer. But the leaders asked for Barabbas to be set free. That's how much they hated Jesus.

At last Pilate gave up. He ordered his soldiers to have Jesus put on a cross to die.

The Roman soldiers put a crown of thorns on Jesus' head. They beat him and made fun of him. At last they led him away to be killed on a cross.

Would you like to give Jesus a hug? Would you like to tell him right now how much you love him? That will be like a hug for Jesus.

Jesus Is Put
on a Cross

Matthew 27:27–56; *Luke* 23:26–49

The Roman soldiers had been beating Jesus. They had pressed a crown of thorns onto his head. They had made fun of him. Now they forced Jesus to drag a big wooden cross through the streets. At last he could drag it no longer. So the soldiers made Simon from Cyrene carry Jesus' cross.

Outside the walls of Jerusalem was a hill called Golgotha. Sometimes it is called Calvary. There the soldiers nailed Jesus' hands and feet to the cross. They set the cross up with Jesus on it.

The religious leaders made fun of Jesus. "Come down from the cross and we'll believe in you," they mocked. On each side of Jesus there was a robber on another cross. One of them made fun of Jesus. The other one believed in him.

For three hours that afternoon the whole world was dark. It was about three o'clock when Jesus cried out, "My God, my God, why have you left me?" Then Jesus shouted again and died.

When Jesus died, the big curtain in God's house, the Temple, ripped into two pieces. The earth shook and rocks tumbled.

Tombs opened and dead believers came back to life. The soldiers were very scared. "Surely this was God's Son," they said.

Many of Jesus' friends watched all of this. There were two women named Mary, and there was the mother of James and John.

What do you suppose these women were thinking?

Jesus
Is Buried

Matthew 27:57–66; *Luke* 23:50–56; *John* 19:38–42

It was about three o'clock in the afternoon when Jesus died. But who was going to bury his body? Where would they bury him?

One of the religious leaders went to Pilate. The leader's name was Joseph. He had come from a place called Arimathea. So he was known as Joseph of Arimathea. Joseph was a member of the group that had asked for Jesus to be killed. But Joseph of Arimathea had not agreed with the others. He believed in Jesus. He had become a secret follower. Now Joseph no longer wanted to keep this a secret. So he asked Pilate if he could bury Jesus in his own tomb.

Joseph's tomb was near Golgotha. It was a big hole that had been cut out of a rock. A big stone, shaped like a coin, covered the opening into the tomb. Joseph was going to place Jesus' body in there. No one had been buried there yet.

So Joseph took Jesus' body down from the cross. He wrapped it in a long, soft cloth. Nicodemus helped Joseph. He was the man who came to see Jesus one night and learned how to be born again. These men put about 75 pounds of spices inside the cloth. That was the way rich people did it at that time.

Joseph and Nicodemus carried Jesus' body to the tomb. They laid it on a stone bench. Then they rolled the big stone over the tomb opening. The two men hurried to finish. It was late on Friday afternoon, and the Sabbath began at sunset on Friday. No one was supposed to work on the Sabbath.

While Joseph and Nicodemus worked, the two women named Mary watched. They were sad that Jesus was dead. But they were happy to see these two men take care of Jesus' body.

You're glad that they did this, too, aren't you?

Some Women
Visit Jesus' Tomb

Mark 16:1–8; Luke 24:1–12

When the sun set on the next evening, which was Saturday, the Sabbath ended. That meant people could begin to work again. So Mary Magdalene and Mary, the mother of James, and several other women went to buy spices. They wanted to put these spices on Jesus' body. But it was dark now, so they could not go to the tomb yet.

As soon as the sun rose on Sunday morning the women went to Jesus' tomb. But they wondered how they were going to get in. Who would roll the big stone away for them?

When they reached the tomb, the women were surprised. The stone was already rolled away from the entrance! So they rushed inside. Jesus' body was gone. The women were confused. What had happened to it?

Then two angels appeared to them. They had shining robes. The robes were so bright that the women could hardly look at them.

"Jesus isn't here," the angels said. "He is alive again! He told you he would

come back to life on the third day. Go back to Jerusalem now and tell the disciples what has happened."

So the women rushed back to Jerusalem. They were shaking. They told the disciples all that had happened.

At first it was hard for everyone to believe that Jesus was alive again. But you believe it, don't you?

Mary Magdalene
Talks to Jesus

John 20:1–18

Peter and John ran to Jesus' tomb. The women had told the disciples it was empty. They had told them about the two angels.

Peter and John wanted to see for themselves. John ran faster. He was there first. He looked into the tomb, but he didn't go in to it.

As soon as Peter got to the tomb, he rushed inside. Then John went in with him. Jesus was gone. But the cloth that had covered Jesus was lying there. The cloth that had covered Jesus' head was folded neatly.

Peter began to wonder. Had Jesus truly risen from the dead? What do you think?

After John went inside and saw the empty tomb, he believed that Jesus really was alive again.

Peter and John went home to Jerusalem.

Then Mary Magdalene came back to Jesus' tomb. She stood there crying. She looked into the tomb again. There she saw two angels in white robes.

One sat where Jesus' head had been. The other sat where Jesus' feet had been.

"Why are you crying?" they asked.

"Because they have taken Jesus' body away," Mary answered. "I don't know where they have put it."

Then Mary looked back and saw that someone was standing behind her. "Why are you crying?" the man asked. "Who are you looking for?"

She thought he was the man who took care of the garden. "Have you taken Jesus away?" she asked. "Tell me where he is. I'll go and get him."

"Mary," the man said. Then Mary knew he was Jesus!

"Teacher!" Mary said. She was so happy and so excited!

"Don't touch me," Jesus told her. "Find the others and tell them that I am going back to heaven."

Mary ran back to the disciples. She told them the wonderful news. "I have seen Jesus!" she said. Then she told them what Jesus had said.

Isn't that wonderful news – that Jesus came back to life? Would you like to tell a friend that Jesus is alive?

Jesus Meets Two People
on the Road to Emmaus

Luke 24:13–35

It was still Sunday, the day when Jesus had come back to life. Two of Jesus' followers were walking to Emmaus. That was a little village 18 kilometres west of Jerusalem. The followers talked about Jesus' death on the cross.

Suddenly Jesus was walking along the road with them. But they didn't know who he was. God kept that a secret.

"You're upset about something," Jesus said. "What's the matter?"

"Terrible things have happened in Jerusalem," one of them answered. His name was Cleopas. "You must be the only one who hasn't heard about them."

"What has happened?" Jesus asked.

"Our Jewish religious leaders arrested Jesus," they said. "Jesus was a great prophet. But our leaders gave him to the Romans, who put him on a cross to die. We thought Jesus was God's Son, the Messiah. We hoped he would save our country, Israel. Now some women have told us his body is missing. They said angels had talked to them. The angels said that Jesus is alive."

"Is it so hard to believe the Scriptures?" Jesus asked. "They say the Messiah must suffer and die." Then Jesus taught them what the Bible said about himself.

At last they came to Emmaus. The two men asked Jesus to come home with them. So he did. When they sat down to eat, Jesus thanked God for the food. Suddenly they knew that he was Jesus! But as soon as they knew, he was gone.

"We felt so warm and wonderful when he talked," Jesus' two followers said. Then they ran back to Jerusalem. This news was too good to keep to themselves.

"Jesus has risen!" the disciples said when the two walked in. "Peter saw him!" Then the two from Emmaus told what had happened to them. Everyone was excited. Jesus was alive! Jesus really had risen from the dead!

Jesus is still alive today. He is living in heaven. That's why he can help us live forever with him. Would you like to say thank you to Jesus now? He's listening!

Jesus Appears
to His Disciples

ᕤᕬ

Luke 24:36–49; *John* 20:19–29

On Sunday night the disciples were together. They were talking with the two followers from Emmaus about the things that had happened that day.

The doors were locked because the disciples were afraid. But suddenly Jesus was there. They thought they must be seeing a ghost.

Jesus said, "Peace be with you." Then he asked, "Why are you afraid? Why do you still doubt that I'm alive? Look at my hands and feet. Touch me! You can't touch a ghost."

The disciples looked at his hands and feet. There were the nail marks. This had to be Jesus. He really was alive! The disciples felt great joy. But they still had some doubts. Was this really and truly Jesus? Was he really and truly alive?

"Do you have something to eat?" Jesus asked. The disciples gave him some broiled fish. They watched him eat it.

Then Jesus taught them what the Scriptures said about him. Moses and the prophets and the writers of the Psalms had all said that Jesus would die and come back to life, just as he did.

"Soon I will send the Holy Spirit to you," Jesus said. "He will give you special power."

Thomas was not there that night. The others told Thomas what had happened. But he would not believe that Jesus was alive. "I must see the nail marks in his hands and feet," Thomas said. "I must touch them."

Eight days later Thomas was with the disciples. The doors were closed and locked. Jesus suddenly appeared again. "Touch my hands and my side," Jesus said to Thomas. "Stop doubting that I'm alive!"

Thomas touched Jesus where the nails had been. "My Lord and my God," Thomas said. Now he believed that Jesus was God's Son and that he was alive.

"Thomas, you believe because you see me," Jesus said. "Many will believe even when they can't see me. They will have a special blessing."

You and I have never seen Jesus. But we believe in him, don't we?

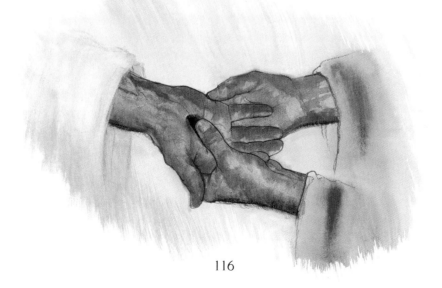

Jesus Helps the Disciples Catch Fish

John 21

Jesus had been alive for more than a week. The disciples went back to Galilee. That's where Jesus had said he would meet them. "I'm going fishing," Peter said one evening. Six other disciples went with him. They sat in their boat and fished all night. But they caught nothing.

As the sun was rising they saw a man standing on the shore of the Sea of Galilee. "Did you catch any fish?" the man asked.

"No, not one," the disciples shouted back.

"Throw your net out on the right side of the boat," the man said. "You will catch plenty of fish there." So that's what the fishermen did. Suddenly their net was full of fish! They could hardly pull it in.

"It's the Lord!" John said to Peter.

So Peter jumped into the water and swam to the place where Jesus was. The others stayed in the boat and rowed it to the shore. Then they pulled the net full of fish out of the water. There were 153 large, heavy fish in it, but the net didn't break.

Jesus had made a fire and was cooking fish on it. He even had bread there for breakfast. "Bring some fish," Jesus said. "Let's have breakfast together."

After breakfast Jesus talked to Peter. "Do you love me, Peter?" Jesus asked.

"Yes," said Peter. "You know I love you."

"Then feed my lambs," Jesus said. He was talking about teaching his followers.

Jesus asked Peter again, "Do you really love me?"

"Yes," said Peter. "You know that I love you."

"Then take care of my sheep," Jesus said.

Once more Jesus asked, "Peter, do you really love me?"

Peter was upset when he heard that. "You know that I do," he answered.

"Then feed my sheep," Jesus said.

What would you say if Jesus asked you, "Do you love me?"

118

Jesus Rises into Heaven

❧

Matthew 28:16–20; *Luke* 24:50–53; *Acts* 1:9–14

One day Jesus met with his disciples. They were on a mountain. Jesus told them about something special he wanted them to do. We sometimes call these words "The Great Commission". This is what Jesus told them to do. He wants us to do it, too.

"I have power in heaven and on earth," Jesus said. "Go to all nations. Teach other people to follow me. Baptise them in the name of God the Father, God the Son, and God the Holy Spirit. Teach them to obey the commands I have given you. Know this for sure! I will be with you always. I will be with you to the end of the world."

At last the time came for Jesus to go back to heaven. That's his home, you know. He came from heaven to be born as a baby in Bethlehem. He lived here on earth for about 33 years. He healed many people. He made demons leave people. He brought dead people back to life. All these things showed that he was God's Son.

Then Jesus died on the cross to take our sins away. On the third day he came back to life.

But now it was time for him to go back home to heaven. So Jesus took his disciples to the Mount of Olives, near the village of Bethany.

Jesus lifted his hands towards the sky. He blessed his followers. Then he began to rise up into the sky. Jesus' friends stood there. They stared at Jesus until he went behind a cloud and they couldn't see him anymore.

Suddenly two angels were standing there with them. "Jesus has gone back to heaven. Someday he will come back the same way that he went," they said. Won't that be a wonderful day?

Then the disciples all went back to Jerusalem. They were so happy that Jesus was coming back again. They went to God's house, the Temple, together. They also met with some others in an upstairs room. They prayed and sang. They waited for the Holy Spirit to come.

The story of Jesus is the most wonderful story ever written. It is the story of God's Son. Jesus loves you very much. He wants everyone to live with him in heaven forever. We know that we will do that someday if we accept him as our Saviour. Would you like to ask him to be your Saviour now?

How to Say Names
of People and Places

PEOPLE

Alphaeus (AL-fee-us)

Barabbas (bur-RAB-us)

Bartimaeus (bar-tih-MAY-us)

Cleopas (KLEE-oh-pus)

Disciples (dih-SIGH-pulls)

Egyptians (ee-JIP-shuns)

Elijah (ee-LIE-jah)

Herod (HAIR-ud)

Iscariot (is-CARE-ee-aht)

Israelites (IS-ray-uh-lites)

Jairus (JIGH-russ)

Lazarus (LAZ-uh-russ)

Magdalene (MAG-duh-lean)

Messiah (muh-SIGH-ah)

Nathanael (nuh-THAN-ee-al)

Nicodemus (nih-koh-DEE-muss)

Pharaoh (FAIR-oh)

Pilate (PIE-lut)

Samaritan (suh-MAR-ih-ton)

Thaddaeus (THAD-dee-us)

Zacchaeus (zak-KEY-us)

Zealots (ZELL-uts)

PLACES

Arimathea (air-ih-muh-THEE-ah)

Bethsaida (beth-SAY-dah)

Cana (CAY-nah)

Capernaum (cuh-PUR-nay-um)

Emmaus (ee-MAY-us)

Galilee (gal-ih-LEE)

Gethsemane (geth-SEM-uh-nee)

Golgotha (GOLL-goh-tha)

Israel (IS-ray-el)

Jericho (JAIR-ih-ko)

Jerusalem (jeh-ROO-suh-lem)

Nazareth (NAZ-uh-reth)

V. Gilbert Beers has written more than 100 books for children, many of which have appeared on best-seller lists.

He is the father of five (one deceased) and the grandfather of eleven.

Gil's passion in life is to help children fall in love with the Bible.

*"If we can help children learn to **love** the Bible, they will love to **learn** the Bible."*

Cheri Bladholm is an award-winning illustrator, she lives in New York with her husband and their two children.